Orangutans

David and Patricia Armentrout

Rourke
Publishing LLC
Vero Beach, Florida 32964

© 2008 Rourke Publishing LLC

All rights reserved. No part of this book may be reproduced or utilized in any form or by any means, electronic or mechanical including photocopying, recording, or by any information storage and retrieval system without permission in writing from the publisher.

www.rourkepublishing.com

PHOTO CREDITS: Cover ©Andy Z; title page, pg. 6, 7, 9, 18 © PhotoDisc; pg. 5 ©Ferry Indrawang; pg. 8 ©Anna Bronshtein Rosenblum; pg. 11 ©Christopher Waters; pg. 12 ©Kitch Bain; pg. 13 ©Christopher Waters; pg. 14 ©Dale Taylor; pg. 15 ©Frank Yuwono; pg. 16 ©Mary Ann Shmueli; pg. 17 ©Andy Z; pg. 19 ©Ecliptic Blue; pg. 20 ©Taolmor; pg. 22 ©A.S. Zain

Editor: Robert Stengard-Olliges

Cover design by: Nicola Stratford, bdpublishing.com

Library of Congress Cataloging-in-Publication Data

Armentrout, David, 1962-
　Orangutans / David and Patricia Armentrout.
　　　p. cm. -- (Amazing apes)
　ISBN 978-1-60044-568-2
　1. Orangutan--Juvenile literature. I. Armentrout, Patricia, 1960- II. Title.
　QL737.P96A757 2008
　599.88'3--dc22
　　　　　　　　　　　　　　　2007010936

Printed in the USA

CG/CG

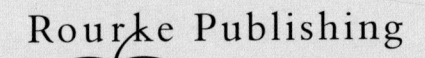

Rourke Publishing

www.rourkepublishing.com – rourke@rourkepublishing.com
Post Office Box 3328, Vero Beach, FL 32964

Table of Contents

Orangutans	4
Please Don't Call Us Monkeys!	6
Heavyweights	9
Life in the Trees	10
Favorite Foods	13
Orangutans Don't Like Crowds	15
Made for Gripping	19
Endangered Species	20
Saving the Amazing Apes	22
Glossary	23
Index	24

Orangutans

Orangutans are large, hairy apes. They have long, powerful arms, reddish brown hair, and human-like faces. The word orangutan means "person of the forest" in the **Malay** language. Orangutans live in rainforests on the islands of Borneo and Sumatra in Southeast Asia. Rainforests are warm, wet forests filled with plants and animals.

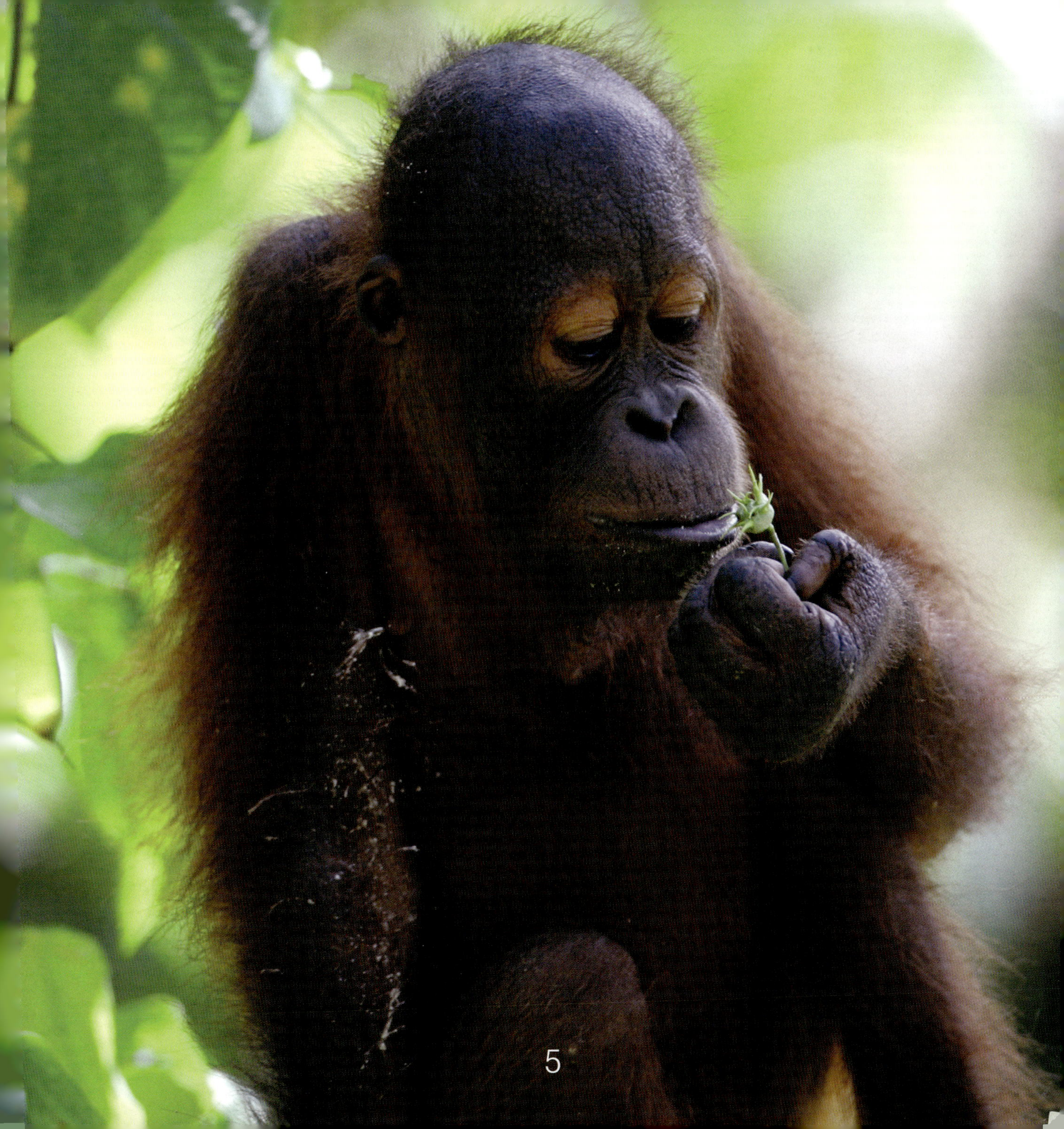

Please Don't Call Us Monkeys!

Orangutans and monkeys share many **traits**. They are both **primates**. They make their homes in the trees and both are expert climbers. But orangutans are not monkeys. Orangutans, along with gorillas and chimpanzees, are part of a group of animals called great apes. Unlike monkeys, great apes have no tail. Great apes are also larger and smarter than monkeys.

Squirrel Monkey

8

Heavyweights

   Female orangutans are much smaller than males. The largest females weigh about 100 pounds (45 kg). Full-grown males can be twice that size at over 200 pounds (90kg). Big males get so heavy that they have trouble swinging from tree to tree and may be forced to walk on the forest floor. Adult male orangutans have large, fleshy cheek pads and a throat pouch that hangs below their chin.

Life in the Trees

Orangutans are **arboreal**, which means they spend most of their lives in trees. They move easily through the forest, swinging from branch to branch with their strong arms and legs. After a long day, orangutans build a nest of leaves and branches high in the treetops for sleeping.

Since orangutans are usually on the move, they build a new nest almost every night.

12

Favorite Foods

The orangutan's favorite food is fruit. Lucky for them, rainforests are home to hundreds of trees, with fruit. When orangutans find a fruit tree, they eat as much as they can. When the fruit is gone, it is time to move on.

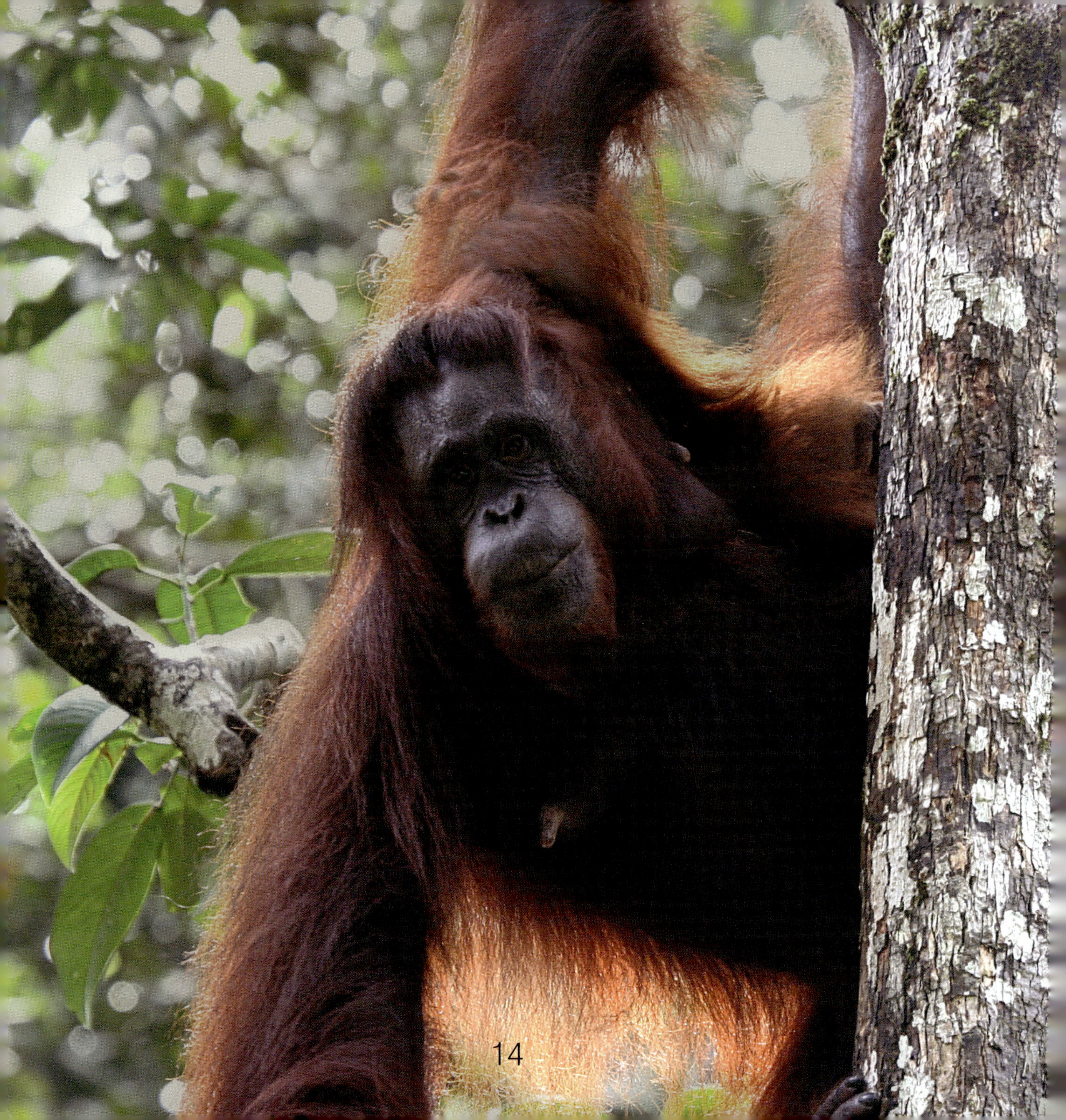

Orangutans Don't Like Crowds

Orangutans like to live alone or in small groups. Adult males prefer to spend most of their time alone. Young females occasionally travel with other young females, but only for a short time.

Mother orangutans are an exception to the rule. They live with and raise their young. **Offspring** stay with their mothers until they are six or seven years old.

Males use their throat pouch to make calls called "long calls" that echo through the forest.

18

Made for Gripping

An amazing feature of orangutans is their hands and feet. Their strong, humanlike hands have four fingers and an opposable thumb. Their feet have four long toes and an opposable big toe. This makes it possible for them to grip with their hands or feet, a big advantage when climbing.

Endangered Species

Orangutans once lived in many parts of Asia, but are now found only on the islands of Borneo and Sumatra. There are so few left that they are an **endangered species**.

Orangutan Habitat

Andaman Sea · *Gulf of Thailand* · *South China Sea* · *Sulu Sea* · *Strait of Malacca* · *Celebes Sea* · *Molucca Sea* · *Java Sea* · *Flores Sea* · *Indian Ocean*

ASIA

Saving the Amazing Apes

Human activity has put the orangutan's survival at risk. But some people are trying to find ways to help these great apes. Scientists and other people who care about orangutans are working to find solutions. If enough people get involved, there may still be time to save the amazing orangutan.

Glossary

arboreal (ar BOR ee ul) — living in trees

endangered species (en DAYN jurd) (SPEE seez) — a species or type of animal that is in danger of becoming extinct

Malay (MAY lay) — a people that inhabit Malaysia and Indonesia

offspring (OFF spring) — an animal's young

primates (PRY maytz) — a group of intelligent mammals that includes monkeys, apes and humans

traits (TRATZ) — a quality or characteristic of an animal or person

Index

Borneo   4, 20
fruit   13
Great apes   6
long calls   17
monkeys   6
opposable   19
rainforest   4
Sumatra   4, 20

FURTHER READING

Orme, Helen. *Orangutans in Danger*. Bearport Publishing, 2006.
Underwood, Deborah. *Watching Orangutans in Asia*. Heinemann, 2006.

WEBSITES TO VISIT

www.worldwildlife.org/apes
nationalzoo.si.edu/Animals/Primates/
www.orangutan.com/index.html

ABOUT THE AUTHOR

David and Patricia Armentrout have written many nonfiction books for young readers. They have had several books published for primary school reading. The Armentrouts live in Cincinnati, Ohio, with their two children.